Men-at-Arms • 72

North-West Frontier
1837–1947

Robert Wilkinson-Latham • Illustrated by Angus McBride

Series editor Martin Windrow

First published in Great Britain in 1977 by Osprey Publishing,
Midland House, West Way, Botley, Oxford OX2 0PH, UK
44-02 23rd St, Suite 219, Long Island City, NY 11101, USA
Email: info@ospreypublishing.com

Osprey Publishing is part of the Osprey Group.

Transferred to digital print on demand 2010

First published 1977
6th impression 2005

Printed and bound by PrintOnDemand-Worldwide.com, Peterborough, UK

A CIP catalogue record for this book is available from the British Library

ISBN: 978 0 85045 275 4

Series Editor: Martin Windrow
Filmset by Great Britain

Artist's note

Readers may care to note that the original paintings from which the colour plates in this book
were prepared are available for private sale. All reproduction copyright whatsoever is retained
by the publishers. All enquiries should be addressed to:

Scorpio
158 Mill Road
Hailsham
East Sussex
BN27 2SH
UK

Email: scorpiopaintings@btinternet.com

The publishers regret that they can enter into no correspondence upon this matter.

The Woodland Trust

Osprey Publishing is supporting the Woodland Trust, the UK's leading woodland
conservation charity, by funding the dedication of trees.

www.ospreypublishing.com

Introduction

For over a hundred years British and Indian troops were engaged on the North-West Frontier of India policing the tribes, mounting expeditions, and guarding the frontier against the ever-present 'threat' from Russia. With the British withdrawal in 1947, the responsibility for continuing this task fell to Pakistan, and many of the problems that beset the British administrators remain to be solved. In 1904 Lord Curzon remarked, 'No man who has read a page of Indian history will ever prophesy about the Frontier.'

The North-West Frontier, or the 'Grim' as it was called by generations of British soldiers, stretched along the borders of Afghanistan and included Little Pamir, Chitral, Kohistan, Bajaur, Khyber, Tirah, Waziristan, and Baluchistan. Though it once belonged to Afghanistan, this tribal territory was inhabited mainly by Pathans, one of the fiercest warrior races on earth, but other tribes, such as the Afridis, the Ghilzais, Baluchis, Waziris, Chitralis, and Kafirs also lived there, and they were all formidable adversaries—ruthless, courageous, and cunning. To be taken alive by the Pathans meant certain agonizing death. Rudyard Kipling expressed the well-founded fears of generations of soldiers:

When you're wounded and left on Afghanistan's
   plains,
An' the women come out to cut up what remains,
Jest roll to your rifle and blow out your
   brains,
An' go to your Gawd like a soldier.

This cruelty did not belong only to the nineteenth century, but continued well into the twentieth.

The British became involved on the North-West Frontier because of the great fear of a Russian invasion through Afghanistan, the 'gateway to India'. Russian influence had, by 1836, reached Persia and she encouraged the Shah to lay siege to Herat in the centre of an Afghan plain often described as the 'granary of Central Asia'.

In 1837 Lord Auckland was appointed Governor-General of India and, soon after taking up his appointment, he sent Captain Burnes, a member of the Honourable East India Company's Political Branch, to Kabul as a special envoy. The Amir Dost Mohomed, who was worried by Persian

1. **Dost Mahomed, the Amir of Afghanistan who was removed from the throne by the British and sent into exile in the Punjab. (National Army Museum)**

2. Afghan soldiers in winter dress. Note the curved stock of the *jezail*, the fur-lined *poshteens*, dagger and pistol. (National Army Museum)

aggression in the west and the constant attacks of the Sikhs in the east, welcomed the Captain with open arms. In return for excluding Russian influence in Afghanistan, the Amir was more than delighted to receive financial aid from Britain; but Burnes had few negotiating powers, and he certainly did not expect the presence of a Russian officer with greater powers on a similar mission, offering financial aid to resist the Sikhs. Britain did not want to offend the Sikhs and therefore refused Burnes bargaining power. By 1838 he had returned to India, the mission having been a total failure.

The Persians, under pressure from the British and facing a threat of war, had abandoned the siege of Herat, thus removing the pressure on the Amir's western borders and the Russian threat to British India. Dost Mahomed was now anxious to resume discussion with the British, but the Council of the Governor-General in Calcutta had already decided to remove the Amir and replace him with Shah Suja, the old ruler of Afghanistan who had been deposed in 1810. The plan to carry this out was evolved by William Henry Macnaghten, chief adviser to Lord Auckland, and it involved the invasion of Afghanistan with the help of Ranjit Singh, the Sikh ruler.

First Afghan War

An army was assembled from elements of the Bombay and Bengal Armies of the Honourable East India Company plus 6,000 recruits for 'the Shah's levies' (Shah Suja). On 10 September 1838 orders were issued for the mobilization of the 'Army of Afghanistan' and, on 1 October, Sir William

Macnaghten issued the Simla Manifesto which summed up the Government's attitude to Afghanistan: 'The welfare of our possessions in the East requires that we should have on our western frontier an ally who is interested in resisting aggression and establishing tranquillity, in the place of chiefs ranging themselves in subservience to a hostile power.'

As this campaign was to be the first of Queen Victoria's reign, failure was unthinkable and so Lord Auckland was instructed by the Court of Directors of the Honourable East India Company to use enough troops to avoid such an occurrence. The instructions continued: 'We are also aware that in carrying out our arms from the Indus we may appear to contemplate schemes of aggrandisement that every consideration both of justice and policy would induce us to condemn, but in truth there is nothing aggressive in what we proposed.' Strange words for men who had decided to remove the ruler of a foreign country by force and replace him with one of their own choosing!

At the beginning of December the huge army with its guns and wagons and 38,000 camp followers started its slow cumbersome march. The first part of the plan was to subdue the amirs of the Sind and to extract from them twenty-five lakhs of rupees (£250,000); this was speedily accomplished by the Bengal Army.

The passage through the Bolan Pass was achieved without any attacks; the army would have suffered badly if the tribesmen had ambushed them. It was at this point that the commissariat arrangements started to break down. The plan for the invasion involved living off the land, but there was little to live off, and the camels carrying the supplies suffered badly on the stony paths; baggage was discarded, and troops were reduced to eating sheepskin cooked in blood, while officers, who still had their personal baggage animals, were enjoying cold meats, game, cheese, port, wine, and whisky. It was obvious that the sooner they reached Kandahar the better and so, leaving the local ruler, the Khan of Khelat, to guard the lines of communication and the Bolan Pass, the army marched on. By the beginning of May the entire force was assembled in Kandahar to await the ripening of the crops. But, in the overcrowded and insanitary city, dysentery and fever soon began to take its toll of the

3. The storming of Ghuznee, the fortress captured through the weakly defended Kabul gate. (National Army Museum)

4. 'The Last Stand of the 44th at Gandamak', a painting by W. B. Wollen. Captain Souter with the Regimental Colour around his waist can be seen to the right of the group. (National Army Museum)

troops. On 27 June Gen. Keane decided to leave a garrison in Kandahar and march on to Kabul.

Between the army and Kabul lay the fortress of Ghuznee, a large forbidding place manned by 3,000 men and with enough supplies to resist a six-month siege. Having left his siege guns as part of the Kandahar garrison, Gen. Keane was undecided what to do. His mind was made up for him by information from an Afghan deserter, who indicated that the weakest point was the Kabul gate of the fortress. On 23 July 1839 sappers blew open the gate with gunpowder charges; within an hour the battle was over, with 1,200 Afghans dead and the rest prisoners.

Dost Mahomed sent his brother Jubbar Khan to negotiate; although he was prepared to submit to Shah Suja, he asked to be made vizir, but his request was refused, and he was eventually exiled to the Punjab.

The army of occupation now settled in and problems soon arose between all parties. Macnaghten assisted by Burnes was in the difficult position of having to persuade the Afghans to accept their new ruler, while at the same time keeping smooth relations with Shah Suja. The great citadel, Bala Hissar, which dominated Kabul was the ideal garrison for the occupying troops, but the British were protectors not conquerors, and in order to maintain the new ruler's prestige in the eyes of his people the cantonments were built outside, on the plain. These were surrounded on all sides by hills and forts, none of which were in British hands, and they had a perimeter of over two miles which could never be adequately defended with the available troops. Perhaps the biggest blunder was to place the commissariat stores a quarter of a mile *outside* the perimeter. These arrangements came in for sharp criticism from some British officers, one of whom was Brig. Abraham Roberts, father of the famous 'Bobs' Roberts of Kandahar. He pointed out to Willoughby Cotton and other commanders that the lines of communication between Kabul and Ghuznee, and Kabul and Kandahar, depended on the goodwill of the local tribes, but he was told that the Ghilzais were co-operating with the East India Company who was paying them a handsome subsidy.

All seemed to be proceeding quietly during 1840. To the north-west of Kandahar the last threat to peace was removed when the Douranee tribes were defeated at little cost. But it was apparent to senior officers that, if the British retired, Shah Suja was doomed, and that stability could only be maintained by means of reinforcements from India.

In the spring of 1841 Willoughby Cotton retired as commander and was replaced by Maj. Gen. William Elphinstone, a kindly man who had last seen military action at the battle of Waterloo twenty-six years previously. Plagued by ill health and limping with gout, his unwillingness and inability to deal with any major problems was another nail in the coffin of the British.

One thing Elphinstone did try and do was improve the position of the cantonments; he recommended the building of a small fort, but this was overruled by the East India Company because of the £2,400 cost. For some time the Board in Calcutta had been worried about the cost of maintaining the army in Afghanistan and some

officials were all for cutting their losses and withdrawing, whatever the consequences. Macnaghton decided to reduce the subsidy paid to the tribes guarding the lines of communication from £8,000—a small sum when the lives of all depended on these tribes—to £4,000. By the beginning of October 1841 the tribes had closed the passes and were attacking any caravan that attempted to pass. Kabul was now cut off from Jalalabad.

The 1st Brigade under Sir Robert Sale, as proof to the Board of the serenity that reigned in Kabul, was ordered to return to India from Kabul via the Khyber Pass, and to scatter the ungrateful Ghilzais. This was accomplished and the brigade then pushed on to Jalalabad, entering it on 13 December 1841.

Kabul displayed little evidence of the calm that Macnaghten, having been offered the governorship of Bombay, was trying to convey to his superiors. At 8.00 a.m. on the morning of 2 November he received an urgent message from Burnes living in the residency inside the city; flames and smoke could be seen, and it was soon confirmed that

5. 'The Remnants of an Army', by Lady Elizabeth Butler. This shows Dr Brydon on a wounded and exhausted horse reaching Jalalabad, 1842.

Burnes, the guards and two officers had all been murdered. The mob then ransacked the paymaster's house, seizing £17,000 and murdering every soldier, camp follower and British dependant they could find.

Elphinstone, as indecisive as ever, wrote calmly to Macnaghten: 'We must see what morning brings and then think what can be done.' While he dithered, the Afghans captured the commissariat fort and another food store on the outskirts of the city. The British inactivity and the repeated successes of the Afghans encouraged more tribesmen to join the uprising. Brig. Shelton, a man of fiery temperament, was itching to deal with the mob, and, had he been allowed to do so at an early stage, the outcome might well have been different. Shelton took positive action and occupied Bala

6. Pathan tribesmen with their long-barrelled *jezails* firing from behind cover on the North-West Frontier. (National Army Museum)

7. Peace negotiations between Amir Ayub Khan (centre) in his resplendent uniform and Sir Louis Cavagnari. Cavagnari was later murdered in Kabul. (National Army Museum)

Hissar, from where he attempted to fire the city with artillery, reasoning that when the Afghans saw their homes burning they would give in, but unfortunately this action had the reverse effect; Shelton and his men were recalled and had to fight their way back to the cantonments. The only hope of reinforcement lay with the 1st Brigade. If they could march on Kabul there was a chance of the rebels being defeated.

After a hastily convened council of war by the 1st Brigade's officers it was decided that, in spite of the messages from Kabul, the state of the troops and supplies, as well as the prospect of leaving the wounded in the dubious care of Afghan irregulars, necessitated a move to Jalalabad leaving a force of Afghan irregulars at Gandamak. The local tribes had so far showed signs of friendship, but as soon as the troops moved out the Afghan irregulars turned on their officers, set fire to the camp, and blew the magazine. At the same time the passes between Sale and Kabul were sealed.

On the 13th Shelton was given a chance to fight and was ordered to dislodge tribesmen occupying the Beymaroo Hills only a few hundred yards from the cantonment, but he mismanaged the attack. As Lady Sale, who watched from the cantonment when the Afghan cavalry charged, wrote in her diary: 'No squares were formed to receive them. All was a regular confusion . . . the onset was fearful. They looked like a great cluster of bees, but we beat them and drove them up again.'

This success was due to the Horse Artillery who nevertheless paid for their temporary triumph—they were obliged to spike and abandon a gun.

The next day Shelton attacked again, this time with his infantry in square formation to receive the attack of the Afghan cavalry. The British field gun fired into the Afghan masses until it overheated and was withdrawn. The Afghan *jezails* outranged the smooth-bore muskets of the soldiers, and the marksmanship of the tribesmen from their secure cover caused a great many casualties. According to Lt. Vincent Eyre, the horse gunner who had cleared the field in Shelton's first attack: 'All have heard of the British squares at Waterloo which defied repeated desperate onsets of Napoleon's choicest cavalry. At Bemaru we formed a square to resist the distant fire . . . thus presenting a solid mass against . . . the best marksmen in the world.'

In vain Shelton ordered the cavalry to charge as

9

8. An Indian field column on the march, 1878–79. This key to an original watercolour by Simkin gives an idea of the disposition of a column on the march in the North-West Frontier areas. (Henry Potter Ltd.)

the tribesmen reinforced the Afghan army but they refused to obey their officers. At last Shelton, wounded in five places, retired slightly to give an order. Imagining that he was deserting his men, the troops broke and, in a confused and jumbled mass of infantry and cavalry, streamed back to the cantonment. 'This,' wrote Shelton himself, 'concluded all exterior operations.' There were now three courses open: to fight it out to the inevitable end; to surrender, which was unthinkable and would terminate Macnaghten's career; or to negotiate in which case Macnaghten might salvage something and possibly save the lives of soldiers and camp followers.

Retreat and Massacre

The first round of talks was unproductive, the Afghans demanding immediate surrender of men and arms. Macnaghten refused, saying, 'We prefer death to dishonour.' At the end of November the favourite son of the exiled Dost Mahomed, Akbar Khan, arrived in Kabul and took charge of the negotiations. Meanwhile the British and sepoy soldiers had to endure the increasing cold, with rations now reduced to the carcases of draft animals. On 11 December Macnaghten, Akbar Khan and a number of Afghan chiefs met and managed to negotiate some form of agreement to the satisfaction of both sides. The British were to leave Kabul for Jalalabad and then return to India, and the garrisons at Ghuznee, Kandahar, and Jalalabad would follow suit.

Macnaghten was still trying to intrigue, using the animosity amongst the various Afghan chiefs to buy time by playing one off against another. Akbar Khan, realizing what he was up to, invited him to a meeting, but no sooner had Macnaghten and three members of his staff dismounted than they were set upon. Macnaghten and an officer were killed and hacked to pieces, and the other two were imprisoned.

With Macnaghten out of the way, the Afghan chiefs imposed sterner terms and demanded of Elphinstone that he leave behind all but six guns, making a large cash payment, and hand over hostages against the safe return of Dost Mahomed.

On 6 January 1842 the retreat began; it was a miserable, freezing column that moved out, consisting of some 4,500 troops, a large number of sick and wounded, stores and baggage, women and children, and about 12,000 camp followers. The order of march was as follows: *Advance Guard:* 44th Foot, Sappers, one squadron Irregular Horse. *Main Column:* two regiments of native infantry, Anderson's Irregular Horse, detachment of Horse Artillery with two guns, women and children with escort. *Rearguard:* two regiments of native infantry;

5th Light Cavalry, remainder of Horse Artillery with four guns. Of this total, 700 were European and the rest native troops.

The reluctance of commanders to allow their men to swathe their legs and feet against the cold resulted in terrible suffering and frostbite especially amongst the native troops; none had eaten a decent meal for some time. They struggled slowly through the snow-covered passes, their numbers being steadily reduced by cold, snipers, and the knives of Afghan raiders. Sepoys threw away their equipment and muskets, Indian mothers threw away their children, and men collapsed with exhaustion, either to freeze where they lay or to fall victim to the harassing tribesmen. On 13 January just over fifty men with only twenty muskets and about fifty rounds of ammunition reached Gandamak; Elphinstone, Lady Sale, MacKenzie and others had been captured by Akbar Khan. The Afghans 'befriended' the survivors and attempted to disarm them. Fighting broke out, and soon only Capt. Souter of the 44th (with the regimental colours tied around his waist), three or four privates, and two civilians remained alive.

Of twelve mounted men who had earlier ridden on to Futtehabad, half had been killed. The Afghans persuaded the remaining six to stop for food and then set upon them; four managed to get away but, as their horses tired, the Afghans killed them one by one until only Surgeon Brydon was left, riding a wounded horse. After two clashes the Afghans lost interest and left Brydon to plod wearily on to Jalalabad, the only European survivor of Elphinstone's 4,500 men. (Later a few sepoys and camp followers completed the journey.)

The immediate result of the disaster was the assembly at Peshawar of a British force. For the next thirty years the frontier simmered—with raids, punitive expeditions, political intrigue between the native rulers and the British—and the

9. G Battery, 3rd Royal Artillery 1879–80. This battery armed with 9-pdr muzzle loaders was part of the Kurram Field Force under General Roberts. Note the short khaki tunics. (National Army Museum)

10. **Sherpur cantonments, 1879, outside Kabul. The troops shown are the 5th Punjab Infantry in winter dress. (National Army Museum)**

shadow of Russian expansion hung everywhere. The timetable of events was as follows:

March
1842   Shah Suja murdered.
April
1842   Akbar's forces defeated at Jal-
                alabad.
September
1842   Afghans defeated at Jungdulluck
                and Tezean. Kabul captured by
                Pollack. Some ninety-five
                prisoners released. Elphinstone
                died in captivity.
December
1842   British and East India Company
                forces evacuate Afghanistan.
January
1843   Dost Mahomed left Lahore for
                Kabul and was restored to the
                throne.
May
1843   Conquest of Sind.

1845–46   1st Sikh War—battles of Mukdi
                (18 Dec. 1845), Ferozeshah
                (21–22 Dec. 1845), Aliwar (28
                Jan. 1846), Sobraon (10 Feb.
                1846). Treaty of Lahore making
                the Punjab a British pro-
                tectorate, 11 March 1846.

December
1849   First armed tax-collecting expe-
                dition.
February
1850   Punitive expedition against Af-
                ridis, who broke their agreement
                to keep the Kohat Pass open.
1851   Captain Coke led expedition
                against Umarzai, Waziris, the
                Black Mountain tribes, and
                others.
1852–53   Five expeditions against trouble-
                some tribes.
1854–55   Three expeditions against trouble-
                some tribes.
1855   Persia seized Herat, British India
                declares war. Treaty swiftly
                negotiated.

1857	Dost Mahomed signs treaty with Sir John Lawrence.
1857–58	Indian Mutiny. Activity on the frontiers.
1859–68	Four expeditions against troublesome tribes.
1863	Ambala Campaign. Death of Dost Mahomed.
1868	Internal troubles in Afghanistan. Sher Ali accepted British subsidy. The start of true 'Russophobia' concerning the North-West Frontier.
1873–74	Expeditions against frontier tribes.
1875	Russia sends enoys to Kabul.
1877	Sher Ali moved troops to the frontier and whipped up feeling against the British.
	Negotiations between British and Afghans. For the first time, large sections of the frontier were mapped in detail. Alternative proposals regarding Afghanistan offered by Lord Lytton:

1 Alliance with Sher Ali

2 Break up Afghanistan and install a puppet amir.

3 Conquer as much of the country as necessary 'for the permanent maintenance of our North-West Frontier'.

Second Afghan War

The threat posed by the Russian presence on the frontier was exacerbated in the 1860s when they annexed the territory of Tashkent, Samarkand, and Khiva. In 1877 Amir Sher Ali received a Russian mission in Kabul; British India immediately demanded equal representation but was refused and, even when the Amir's subsidy was cut off, he refused to yield. In 1878 he signed a treaty with the Russians. With a touch of imperial arrogance it was decided that a mission should be sent to the Afghans; it set out under an armed escort but was turned back at the Khyber Pass. An ultimatum was despatched demanding an apology and threatening invasion if it was not forthcoming. At the same time an army was assembled, sparing

11. A signal section attached to the Kurram Field Force. The soldiers, not in khaki, are standing round an Engineer, who is sending a message in morse. On the left is Mr Josephs, the civilian Superintendent of Telegraphs, and on the right natives with wire ready for laying. (National Army Museum)

12. **The Bala Hissar gate, 1879, with troops outside. Inside Bala Hissar fortress was the Amir's palace and also the British residency which was stormed and burned in September 1879.**

no expense, for the invasion of Afghanistan. It was divided into three field forces—the Peshawar Valley Field Force under Lt. Gen. Sam Browne, designer of the belt that bears his name; the Kandahar Field Force under Maj. Gen. Donald Stewart; and the last and smallest under Maj. Roberts who was given a local rank of major general.

At 3.00 a.m. on 21 November 1878, with the ultimatum unanswered, Robert's force crossed the border into Afghanistan. Unfortunately the Peshawar Valley Field Force had the best troops, whereas Robert's force consisted of one British regiment of young, newly-arrived troops, six native regiments, and the 5th Gurkhas, who were his best troops. He received reinforcements of some extra artillery, some Sikhs, and a part of the 72nd Highlanders. Advancing down the Kurram Valley, he approached Peiwar Kotel where the Afghan army had positioned itself The pass was narrow and well defended and, towering above it, was a strongly fortified mountain. Roberts waited in front of the pass for several days and amassed what information he could about the enemy numbers and positions before deciding on a desperate plan. He had gun positions built so that the enemy thought he was about to launch a frontal assault;

then, on the night of 2 December, he marched round the left flank of the forbidding mountain and assaulted the Afghans, who were (unusually for them) completely taken by surprise; they retreated immediately, leaving the way open.

After a suitable rest, and having received large reinforcements of men and munitions, he pushed forward to the end of the Kurram Valley, establishing a firm line of communication. As most of the telegraph lines had been cut by the Afghan tribesmen, heliographs were set up as a second line of communication.

On 7 January an incident occurred in Roberts's camp that did no credit to the war correspondents and brought Roberts, as he later wrote, 'into disrepute with one of the leading London newspapers'. The enemy were discovered trying to creep into the camp and 'at the sound of the first shot the prisoners all jumped to their feet, and calling each other to escape, attempted to seize the rifles belonging to the guard'. Fearing for the safety of his men, he gave the order to fire; six prisoners were killed and thirteen wounded. Roberts had already warned MacPherson of *The Standard* about his abuse of the favours Roberts had shown the Press. 'Judging from his telegrams,' wrote the General, 'which he brought to me to sign, the nerves of the correspondent in question must have been somewhat shaken by the few and very distant shots fired at us on 28 November. These telegrams being in many instances absolutely incorrect, and of the most alarming nature, were not of course allowed to be despatched until they were revised in accordance with the truth.' MacPherson composed one about the prisoner incident and sent it without showing it to Roberts, who saw it for the first time in *The Standard* when the paper arrived in Kurram. In Parliament the incident was represented on *The Standard*'s authority as the slaughter of ninety prisoners tied together with ropes. 'What to my mind,' Roberts wrote strongly, 'was so reprehensible in the correspondent's conduct was the publication in time of war, with consequent excitement and anxiety at home, of incorrect and sensational statements, founded on information derived from irresponsible and uninformed sources.'

The war ended when Sher Ali fled to Russia; his

13. Lord Roberts wearing an Afghan *poshteen*, suitable for the cold climate of the North-West Frontier. (Parker Gallery)

son Ayub Khan became the new ruler and he was anxious that 'the friendship of this God-granted State with the illustrious British Government may remain constant and firm'. On 26 May the Treaty of Gandamak was signed, which allowed a British envoy in Kabul, ceded territory to India, and established telegraph lines between the Afghan

capital and Indian frontier; Britain was to control Afghan foreign policy and in return promised protection from aggression. Seemingly, the Russian threat to India had been reduced. In May 1879 Sir Louis Cavagnari was installed as the British resident at Kabul.

The second phase of the Second Afghan War was sparked off by the murder of Cavagnari and his staff at Kabul. The only British force in Afghanistan was the old Kurram Field Force under Roberts, which was employed on police duties. This was immediately reinforced, renamed the Kabul Field Force, and ordered to advance on the Afghan capital to exact retribution. Howard Hensman, the special correspondent of the *Pioneer*, Allahabad, and the *Daily News*, London, wrote: 'It was my good fortune to be the only special correspondent with the gallant little army which moved out of Ali Khedyl in September 1879. The Government of India [presumably after the affair of MacPherson of *The Standard*] had announced that "noncombatant correspondents" would not be allowed to join the force.'

The Field Force moved up the Kurram Valley, winning a number of small encounters with the enemy. Amir Ayub Khan was in constant contact with Roberts, denying responsibility for the murder of the British envoy and entreating the British not to invade. By the beginning of October 1879 Roberts's force was twelve miles from the capital, at Charasia, where 8,000 Afghans had entrenched themselves. With a force of 7,500 and twenty-two guns Roberts had driven the tribesmen off the ridge and was preparing for his final advance to Kabul. Hensman described the scene of the formal occupation of the city and the triumphant parade of the British and Indian troops, infantry, cavalry, artillery, and Sappers and Miners. 'Nothing could exceed the splendid form in which these regiments turned out, the bronzed and bearded faces of the soldiers showing but few "six-year men" [this new term of enlistment was introduced in 1870, replacing the previous one, which was for twenty-one years] were in their ranks. . . . The sight was a most impressive one, the sun lighting up the double line along which 4,000 bayonets sparkled, and throwing into bold relief the darker forms of men and horses where the cavalry were drawn up.' Hensman was of the opinion that 'there was nothing to hinder us marching into the fortress the day after the battle of Charasia. . . . But there was no occasion for haste.'

On 10, 11, and 12 November the forty-nine 'murderers' of the Kabul envoy were found guilty by a military commission, and hanged as an example to others. To hold Kabul, as Roberts well knew, would not be so simple. The Afghans were by nature independent and cunning, and they did not know when they were beaten. In December 10,000 Afghans rose against the invader, marching in small armies on Kabul. Just before Christmas their attention turned on Roberts's force, but he was so well prepared that the Afghan army was repelled at the battle of Sherpur. By March 1880 the British had strengthened their position and Maj. Gen. Sir Donald Stewart had moved a force to Kandahar under Maj. Gen. Primrose before marching on Kabul with 14,000 extra troops.

At the end of June reports reached Kandahar that Ayub Khan was marching on it with a large army intent on its capture. A force under Gen.

Burrows, comprising 500 cavalry, six horse artillery guns, infantry consisting of the 66th Regiment and 1st Bombay Grenadiers, and various other troops and services, marched to Maiwand on 27 July to intercept Ayub Khan's army, and the disastrous action took place which resulted in the siege of Kandahar. In September Hensman filed what he claimed was the first unofficial account of the disaster of Maiwand. The British loss was more than 1,000 fighting men killed, over a quarter being from the 66th Regiment, and 175 wounded or missing. Roberts was instructed to relieve Kandahar, and on 9 August he marched out of Kabul with a force of nearly 10,000 combatants. Twenty days later Hensman wired his report, stating that 'more than 300 miles have been covered, giving an average (including one day's halt) of fifteen miles per day. I will leave it to military criticism to decide as to the merits of such a march.'

On 1 September 1880 Roberts finally thrashed Ayub Khan's army and captured numerous men and stores, thus virtually ending the war. A new amir was placed on the throne and Britain withdrew her armies to India, a rather un-

14. **Tribesmen lying in ambush for an Indian or British column; one or two are armed with Enfield, or probably Snider-Enfield breech-loaders, while others still have the** *jezails.* **The one in the foreground has a rest for accurate sniping. (National Army Museum)**

satisfactory end to the campaign. A campaign medal was struck for participants, including Roberts's horse and a small white mongrel named Bobbie, the pet of the 66th (in 1881, 2nd Bn Royal Berkshire Regiment) who had 'served' through the entire war and had been at Maiwand.

One result of the campaign in Afghanistan was the setting up, at Kabul in 1881, of a committee to consider the suitability of equipment for troops on active service. It recommended a new type of equipment for infantry (the Slade Wallace equipment, which was similar to that recommended, was adopted in 1888) but turned most of its attention to the cavalry and the manner in which carbine and sword were carried. The sword was needed most when the user was mounted, so it was decided to fit it into a frog on the shoe case; the carbine, however, would be used when the owner was dismounted and so it could be slung on a specially designed cross-belt. This idea was later adopted as the Patterson equipment.

A pro-British Afghan government was established under Abdur Rahman, cousin of Sher Ali, and the British finally withdrew in 1881. No sooner had they gone than Ayub Khan made another bid for power; he defeated the army sent by Abdur Rahman, and captured Kandahar on 27 July, but two months later he had to flee to Persia, after Abdur Rahman had defeated him on 22 September.

In March 1885 Russian troops, having occupied Merv the previous year, crossed the disputed frontier with Afghanistan and fought the Afghan army. Britain's clear determination to side with the Afghans averted what would have been a full scale war.

| 1888 | Black Mountain or Hezara expedition undertaken after the murder of two officers and five sepoys engaged on survey work in territory occupied by the Akazais. |
| 1891 | Further expeditions against the Hassanzais and Akazais in the Black Mountain. |

15. The charge of the 9th (Queen's Royal) Lancers at Kandahar on 1 September 1880 with the Afghans in full flight. (Parker Gallery)

Chitral, Malakand and Tirah

16. **The Amir Sher Ali, photographed in 1880. (National Army Museum)**

Britain had unwittingly become involved in the affairs of the small state of Chitral as far back as 1876 when pressure from powerful neighbours caused the Chitralis to place themselves under the protection of the Maharaja of Kashmir, who was himself under the protection of the Government of India.

Intrigue at court and the assassination of one ruler after another had created a chaotic situation when the British finally recognized Nizam-ul-Mulk. Surgeon Major Robertson was despatched to Chitral as Political Agent, but no sooner had he arrived than Nizam-ul-Mulk was murdered by his brother Amir-ul-Mulk who installed himself on the throne. Robertson recognized the new ruler in January 1895, when he returned to the capital with an escort of a hundred men of the 14th Sikhs and 300 Kashmiri light infantry. In March Robertson removed Amir-ul-Mulk from the throne and replaced him with his twelve-year-old son Suja-ul-Mulk. But the boy's uncle, Sher Afzal, had designs on the throne and he assembled an army to stake his claim by force. He was joined by Umra Khan, the ruthless ruler of Jandol, which lay south of Chitral, and the first contact with the Indian troops was outside Chitral. Robertson sent 250 Kashmiris to reconnoitre, but they were severely mauled by Sher Afzal's army; their worn-out Snider-Enfields were almost smooth-bored and were no great aid to their shooting ability. But the casualties would have been higher than the fifteen killed and forty wounded had the Sikhs not covered their disorderly flight back to the fort. On 4 March 1895 the siege of Chitral started with 343 fit for duty (eighty-three Sikhs, fifty-two doubtful Chitralis, and the rest consisted of badly-armed Kashmiris). Ammunition was fairly plentiful and there was food, though it was mostly pea flour, which meant that throughout the siege pea soup was a daily dish.

The following day Lts. Edwards and Fowler set off from Mastuj, sixty miles north-east of Chitral, with an escort of sixty men and porters carrying ammunition for Chitral. When they reached the fortified village of Reshun the Chitralis appeared to

1893	Establishment of the Durand Line, which gave rise to problems on the North-West Frontier; several independent states were divided by the line and belonged neither to India nor to Afghanistan.
1894–95	Punitive expedition to Waziristan to deal with repeated attacks by Waziris on the Afghan Frontier Delimitation Party. First campaign in which the Lee-Metford rifle with cordite cartridges was used.

welcome them, announced a polo match and invited the two officers. After the match the officers were seized and the leaderless soldiers were overpowered and slaughtered.

Reports of the siege had filtered through to Peshawar, where a large force of some 15,000 men and 20,000 animals were assembled under Maj. Gen. Sir Robert Low. Unfortunately its enormous size caused it to move at a snail's pace. On 7 April the army fought its first battle and forced the Malakand Pass by an outflanking movement of the Guides and Sikhs which allowed the Gordons and the King's Own Scottish Borderers to storm the crest at bayonet point.

While this force was slowly fighting its way towards Chitral a smaller force under Lt. Col. James Kelly of the 32nd Sikh Pioneers consisting of 416 men and porters and two 7-pdr outdated mountain guns set out from Gillait on 27 March. The men suffered from the snow and cold and their rate of advance slowed to a mile per hour; gorges had to be crossed without the aid of bridges, as the enemy had destroyed them. Finally on 20 April, after the garrison of Chitral had successfully stifled a mining operation by a sortie of volunteers, Kelly and his men were able to build a bridge over the last vital gorge and relieve the town. The force had marched 220 miles and fought two battles in twenty-eight days in appalling conditions. Low and his mammoth force arrived one week later to find their task accomplished by an officer with Sikh Pioneers and Kashmiri Sappers. Low's troops, however, went on to rescue Edwards and Fowler, who were released by Umra Khan in a belated act of appeasement. The campaign ended with the usual Queen's message and the rewards to officers of knighthoods and decorations. For his brilliant march Kelly received a CB and promotion to full colonel.

The numbers of men and guns which the tribes could put into the field were fairly formidable. In 1884 Lt. Col. W. Paget's *A Record of the Expeditions against the North-West Frontier* listed the estimated strengths of the various tribal groups. The 'Northern tribes'—Kanjutis, Chitralis, Chilasis and Kohistanis—mustered a total of some 22,000 men, a minimum of 12,000 matchlocks and flintlocks, several small batches of Berdan, Snider, and Martini-Henry rifles, and several 6-pdr or 7-pdr

cannon. The three main groups of Pathan tribes were the Isazai Yusufzais with 5,700 men and some 3,600 firearms of elderly types; the Ilaszai Yusufzais with roughly 30,000 men could field a

17. Sowar, 11th Bengal Lancers, circa 1886. Note the leather equipment with carbine slung on the cross-brace on his back and the stirrup-hilted sword in a frog at his left side. (National Army Museum)

majority of warriors with firearms of some type; while the Mandan Yusufzais had 2,000 men of whom two-thirds carried firearms. Allied tribes such as the Swatis, Mohmands, etc. numbered in all some 50,000 men of whom about half had guns.

18. Havildar, 1st Central India Horse, with a different pattern of equipment and a three-bar-hilted sword; note the butt of the lance also differed from the British pattern. (National Army Museum)

The eleven main Afridi tribes totalled some 60,000 men with a couple of hundred magazine rifles, some 6,500 Enfields, and about 40,000 matchlocks. The five Waziri tribes totalled more than 50,000 men, some half of them with firearms; and although firearm figures were not available it may be assumed that the 23,000-odd men of the nine Baluchi tribes were armed in about the same proportion. This gave a total for the whole vast and inaccessible region of no less than 240,000 men—which in Frontier terms meant 240,000 fearless and bloodthirsty warriors—of whom half had guns of some kind. One may be sure that Europeans with experience of Frontier fighting would regard the remainder, armed with cold steel, with very real respect.

The weakness of the Frontier peoples was, of course, their lack of unity. Inter-tribal raiding and a constant state of shifting alliances and intermittent warfare was their whole way of life: British and Indian Army forces of a fraction of their total strength could normally achieve local superiority without much difficulty—though always at the expense of sharp and bloody little battles in nameless places. It was thus all the more ominous when, in Queen Victoria's diamond jubilee year of 1897, a fanatical uprising occurred in the Swat Valley led by a holy man styled the Mad Mullah. From Baluchistan to the Swat the tribes rose *en masse* as the Mullah's influence spread. He achieved a measure of unity among them by preaching that Britain was crumbling, that Christianity itself was reeling; he also claimed that Britain had lost Suez and Aden, and was therefore unable to reinforce her army in India.

Britain's answer was to appoint Maj. Gen. Sir Bindon Blood to command the Malakand Field Force. He successfully led his force against the tribesmen and defeated them at Chakdara and in the Upper Swat, but even his efforts could not contain the tribes. They swept down from Swat to the Khyber Pass, along to Kohat, up the Kurram Valley, and south to Baluchistan. Soon, isolated forts and garrisons fell to the Pathans and on 25 August 1897—the blackest day of Frontier history—the British lost control of the famed Khyber Pass. Queen Victoria telegraphed the Secretary for India that 'These news from the Indian frontier are most distressing . . . am most anxious to know the names of those who have fallen. What a fearful number of officers!'

By the end of the summer, field forces were operating in Swat Valley, Tochi Valley, and a third was fighting the Mohmands. The situation was confusing and the Queen admitted that she had to rely on the newspapers for accurate information.

This situation was not new: in 1879 Disraeli had written to Lady Chesterfield, 'The Afghan news is very good and I credit it; but, strange to say, the Government has not yet had any telegram confirming it. But we cannot compete with *The Standard* newspaper which does not hesitate to expend £500 on a telegram!'

The loss of the Khyber was a severe blow to Imperial prestige and it was decided to attack the Afridis, the largest and most troublesome of the tribes. Sir William Lockhart was recalled to take command of the punitive Tirah expedition. His force consisted of 44,000 troops and 60,000 transport animals plus mountain artillery and rockets. On 18 October 1897 the first clash with the Pathans took place at Dargai, and a second a few days later. With an estimated 12,000 tribesmen holding the heights, all well concealed behind stone sangars, the 2nd Gurkhas, the Derbyshire Regiment, and the Dorsetshire Regiment attacked up a 300-yard slope towards a narrow footpath leading to Dargai. For five hours they endured the accurate rifle fire of the tribesmen, as well as a hail of stones and rocks, in an attempt to reach the footpath. Then the 3rd Sikhs and the Gordon Highlanders were ordered up, as it was thought that Dargai had to be taken at all costs so as to maintain Imperial prestige.

After a short artillery barrage, with the pipes playing, the Gordons made a dash up the slope under murderous fire. Amongst the many casualties was Piper Findlater who was shot through both legs, but he propped himself against a rock and continued playing, for which he was awarded the Victoria Cross. The Gordons cleared the slope, then the cliff, and were joined by the 3rd Sikhs and the remnants of the first assault in taking Dargai.

The army continued its march to Tirah, taking the Sempagha Pass on 29 October after feeble resistance of the tribe, then the Arhanga Pass on the 31st, and the army passed into the Maidan Valley where they set about punishing the tribes by burning villages and destroying crops.

Since the attack on Malakand the British had suffered 1,300 casualties.

The tribes were temporarily subdued, but few paid the fines of handing in rifles (1907 were demanded, 89 received). Had it all been worth it?

19. Rifleman, 3rd Gurkhas. The uniform was green with black leather equipment; note the expense pouch hanging to the right beneath the belt. (National Army Museum)

the Khyber Pass was recaptured; later in the month the Afridis surrendered and agreed to pay their fines. But all who had been connected with the Frontier knew that it was only a pause in the fighting.

During the reign of Queen Victoria the numerous expeditions on the Frontier were rewarded by the India General Service Medal 1854–95 with the bar 'North-West Frontier' for sixteen expeditions between 1849 and 1868, the Afghan war medals and the India Medal 1895–1902 with seven possible bars. Between 1908 and 1939, two medals were issued: the India General Service Medal 1908-35 with eight bars and the India General Service Medal 1936–39 with two bars.

In 1903 Russia again sent agents into Afghanistan so the British Foreign Office sent a strong note but the Russian ambassador in London opened discussions with the British Government. In August 1907 a convention was signed in St Petersburg which laid down that Afghanistan was outside the Russian sphere of influence and that Britain would neither annex territory nor meddle in internal affairs. With this historic convention, the so-called 'great game' was over though not the Frontier troubles, which continued until after the British left in 1947.

Third Afghan War

The death in 1901 of Amir Abdur Rahman led indirectly to the Third Afghan War; his successor, Amir Habibullah Khan, was an unreliable and unstable man who alternately sided with Britain and Russia according to the subsidy each gave. During the First World War the Amir accepted a Turkish military mission and military equipment, which soon became a Turco-German mission. This displeased Britain on two counts; Germany was her enemy and she had been given responsibility for Afghanistan's foreign affairs by the Treaty of Gandamak in 1879.

When the mission left in 1916 it had succeeded in planting in the Amir's mind the idea that Afghanistan was an independent nation; in 1919 he demanded participation in the Versailles Treaty, but was refused by the Viceroy. Eighteen days later the Amir was killed on a shoot and his eldest son,

20. Lance naik, 11th Bengal Native Infantry, 1886. The scarlet tunic had a central stripe in the facing colour and cuffs in the facing colour. The 'valise' equipment was in brown leather. (National Army Museum)

Queen Victoria thought not when she wrote to the Viceroy, 'As we did not wish to retain any part of the country, is the continuation and indefinite prolongation of these punitive expeditions really justifiable at the cost of many valuable lives?' The fighting continued, however, and on 7 March 1898

who was not a strong character, proclaimed himself Amir. But in Kabul Amanullah Khan, the third son, had already proclaimed himself Amir; unfortunately the army suspected his complicity in the death of his father and, in order to create a diversion, he decided to invade India. He enlisted the aid of dissident Indian revolutionaries, and in Peshawar the postmaster, an Afghan leader of the Peshawar Union Committee, was used to distribute inflammatory leaflets, one of which stated, 'You should therefore use every possible means to kill British, continue to tear up railways and cut down the telegraph.'

The attack had been timed to coincide with a rising in the Punjab which occurred on 10 April, when looting, fire, rape, and arson took place in Amritsar, and in Lahore only military intervention restored order. Telegraph wires were cut and the revolt spread. On 13 April at Amritsar Brig. Gen. Dyer learned that, in spite of orders, a large political meeting was to take place in an enclosed area called the Jallianwala Bagh. Knowing that agitators would incite the crowd to murder and violence and that he had a pitifully small force to protect the European community, he marched his fifty men into the Bagh and opened fire, killing 379 and wounding 1,500. Within a few days the Punjab rising had died down, without the Afghan attack having taken place. But their troops were already moving towards the frontier, with a concentration in the Khyber district, and the Indian Government ordered a general mobilization, declaring war on 6 May.

The following day the small British force at Landi Kotal was reinforced by the Somerset Light Infantry (who were smuggled past the tribesmen in covered lorries), and war began in earnest on the 8th. It could not have happened at a worse time; with the end of the First World War, troops were exhausted and disenchanted. Those in India, mostly reserves and territorials, were anxious for demobilization, while the line regiments were all due for home service. The Indian Army, which had sent overseas more than a million men, was also tired; and the whole war machine of the Empire was at a very low ebb when the Afghans chose to attack. On 11 May 1919 an attack was launched o the Afghans at Landi Kotal; it was supported by machine guns, and after thirty minutes of bombardment, the Afghans were driven towards the Lower Khyber and were caught in an intensive fire from the mountain batteries. No counter-attack was launched as the tribesmen were more preoccupied with picking up the Afghan rifles and ammunition.

1919

13 May	British and Indian troops take western Khyber with no opposition.
16 May	British attack 'Stonehenge Ridge'. After preliminary bombardment, Sikhs attacked but were halted at 8.00 a.m. when ammu-

21. The full-dress splendour of the Indian cavalry, shown in this watercolour by Chater Paul Chater of a native officer of the 15th Cureton's Multanis. (Wilkinson-Latham)

22. Havildar Major (sergeant major) of the Corps of Guides by Chater Paul Chater. (Wilkinson-Latham)

nition ran out. At 10.30 a.m. ammunition arrived and an attack opened at 2.00 p.m. in intense heat. After bombardment, the line attacked and reached the top of the deadly escarpment to find that the Afghans had retired leaving equipment, guns and standards.

23 May   Fight in eastern Khyber and raids by Afghans. British posts in Kurram Valley abandoned. Desertion amongst North Waziristan Militia. South Waziristan Militia also deserted so militia posts abandoned. The militia, it

was realized, was more of a liability than an asset. At Wana, militia attack British officers and loyal men who fought their way out.

24 May   Kabul bombed by Handley-Page bombers. Troops were living on tinned meat and biscuits as there was no fresh meat or vegetables. Of the 'bullied mutton' from Australia one officer wrote, 'The gentleman who produced it had, rashly, put his portrait on the tins and many people kept these labels hoping that in the future they might meet him.'

27 May   Attack by Afghan troops with artillery on Thal failed. Frontier constabulary decamped, allowing Afghans to occupy tower 500 yards from fort and burn food dumps.

1 June   Relief force under Brig. Gen. Dyer reached Darsaman, nine miles from Thal. Following day Dyer launched attack at first light which was still in progress when Afghans approached H.Q. under flag of truce. They delivered a message saying that the Amir Amanullah had ordered Nadir Khan to suspend hostilities. Nadir Khan asked for acknowledgement. Dyer did not know that the Amir had requested the Indian Government for an armistice on 31 May, but unwilling to take any chances he gave his famous answer, 'My guns will give an immediate reply, but your letter will be forwarded to the Divisional Commander.' The attack continued but the Afghans withdrew and Dyer ordered lancers supported by armoured cars to advance and harass the enemy. Further north, aerial attack by the R.A.F. dispersed tribesmen.

1 Sergeant, Bengal Horse Artillery, 1842
2 Captain, 44th Foot, 1842
3 Private of battalion company, 44th Foot, 1842

Angus McBride

A

1 Officer, 3rd Light Dragoons, 1842
2 Private, 13th Foot, 1842
3 Sepoy, Light Company, 35th Bengal
  Native Infantry, 1842

B

Angus McBride

1 Private, 10th Hussars, 1879
2 Officer, 18th Foot attached
   Commissariat, Kabul, 1880
3 Infantry officer, 1879

Angus McBride

C

1 Officer, Royal Horse Artillery, 1879
2 Sowar, 12th Bengal Cavalry, 1888
3 Havildar, Mountain Artillery Battery, 1899

D

Angus McBride

1 Private, British Infantry, 1897
2 Havildar, 30th Punjab Infantry, 1897
3 Sowar, 10th Bengal Lancers, 1897

Angus McBride

E

1 War correspondent, 1897
2 Private, 1st Gordon Highlanders, 1908
3 Officer, South Wales Borderers, 1937

F

Angus McBride

1 Highland Guard, Afghan Army, 1879
2 Cavalry trooper, Afghan Army, 1879
3 Amir Ayub Khan, 1880

Frontier tribesmen

H

Angus McBride

3 June	Afghan camp at Yusef Khel, which was empty, seized. Armistice signed.
8 August	Peace treaty of Rawalpindi signed.

Rumours spread amongst the Waziris and Mahsuds that Britain was going to hand Waziristan to the Amir and this encouraged the tribes to start raiding on a large scale in the administered areas. By November they had killed 225 and wounded a further 200. The British immediately held a number of *jirgas* (tribal gatherings) to explain that Waziristan was not to be handed over but that roads would be built and troops stationed in protected areas. This had little effect, and ferocious fighting continued until March 1924.

In the following years the large self-contained fortress of Razmak capable of holding 10,000 men was completed and a second camp established at Wana. New roads were constructed giving speedier troop movements, but the tribesmen could still attack and swiftly disappear over the Durand Line before troops could intercept them. However, with the establishment of the camps and the use of columns for patrolling, raiding almost ceased.

By 1930, with a change of ruler in Afghanistan, the threat of Russia removed and a peaceful frontier, a new era of Anglo-Afghan co-operation seemed imminent.

Abdul Ghaffar Khan had been known to the British since 1919 when he agitated against the Rowlatt Act, which retained the powers taken during the war for peacetime. Political agitation was rife during the 1920s beyond the Indus because of the Montagu-Chelmsford reform which introduced dualism as a step to responsible government by Indians but this was not extended to the Pathans. Ghaffar Khan preached that the Pathans were being insulted by this blatant discrimination. After coming out of jail in 1920 he joined Gandhi's National Congress party and, in 1929, he formed his 'Khudai Khitmatgers' with young Pathans, to fight against British rule. Because they were poor and could not afford uniforms, shirts were dyed in brickdust, which earned them the popular nickname of 'The Red Shirts'. Units were organized on a military basis with drill training and badges of rank; Ghaffar Khan even published his own drill manual. For some unexplained reason the authorities allowed the 'Red Shirts' to prosper. Ghaffar Khan toured the frontier areas preaching violence to the tribes, telling them that British power was failing and that their Indian army would not fight on the British side much longer. In Peshawar, on 20 April, a large gathering took place, attended by representatives of the frontier areas and large units of 'Red Shirts' with bands and banners. Finally it dawned on the authorities that some form of uprising was not too far away; from 4.00 p.m. on 23 April a 'City Disturbance Column' was created, and was ready to move at thirty minutes' notice.

Two days after the meeting Ghaffar Khan and a number of his followers were arrested, but on their way to the jail the mob slashed the lorry tyres and attempted to free the prisoners. The prisoners and

23. **Native officer of the Central India Horse in full dress far more resplendent than the *sowar* shown in figure 17.**

their escort, however, made their way to jail on foot. In other parts of the city too, the mob was becoming violent and a request was made by the Deputy Commissioner for the 'City Disturbance Column'. The Deputy Commissioner then tried to make his way through the Kabul Gate with four armoured cars but these were attacked by the crowd with bricks. Two motorcyclists following the column were set upon and one was killed. Immediately the leading armoured car moved to cover the body, and was itself attacked. Permission was given for the armoured cars to open fire which they did, pursuing the mob. Once the mobile column arrived the side streets were sealed off but the mob attacked again and tried to set fire to the armoured cars. Forbidden to fire, the troops formed a cordon round the armoured car. One soldier was badly hit and dropped his rifle; an Indian VCO attempted to retrieve it and was set on by the crowd, so he fired. With the situation rapidly deteriorating, permission was given to open fire

and the streets were soon cleared by the troops. The army occupied the city on the 24th, but a deputation of elders begged the Chief Commissioner to remove the troops, promising that they would then guarantee peace. The offer was accepted but peace was short-lived, the 'Red Shirts' erected a memorial and, on 19 May, this was demolished.

1930

13 May	Ultimatum issued by the British demanding disbandment and delivery of twenty hostages.
14 May	No answer received. RAF attacked two villages, killing seven people and destroying thirty houses.
15 May	Razmak column reached Madda Khel but tribes had disappeared. Twenty hostages surrendered themselves. There was also trouble in Tirah and elsewhere, stirred up by 'Red Shirts' agents.

24. Two men of the Gordon Highlanders on guard outside Fort Jamrud. (Wilkinson-Latham)

5 June	Large numbers of Afridis marching on Peshawar were harassed by RAF. During the night telephone wires were cut and Indian patrols fired on. Flying column formed of Guides, 20th Lancers and squadron of 15th/19th Hussars, who swept along the line of the river but found no large groups of tribesmen; these men later machine-gunned and bombed by the RAF.
16 August	Martial law proclaimed in Peshawar district.
October	After prolonged negotiations, settlement was made, allowing Afridis to enlist in the Indian Army and giving Britain the right to over-fly Tirah and patrol the plains.
1931 March	Ghaffar Khan released from jail. 'Red Shirts' attempt to disrupt civil court cases and subjects

25. With tribesmen indulging in their favourite pastime of telegraph wire cutting, the heliograph was a vital item of equipment; it is being used here by men of a cavalry regiment at Fort Hari-Sing. Note their quilted neck flaps. (Wilkinson-Latham)

	loyal to Britain persecuted.
23 December	Emergency powers taken to protect the public services, property and order. 'Red Shirts' declared illegal.
28 December	Last British troops withdrawn from Peshawar city.

By the spring of 1932 the 'Red Shirts' had disappeared, and in 1935 the North-West Province was raised to the status of a Governor's province, with political rights equal to those of the rest of India.

The Last Years

The Government had now decided that there should be certain 'rules' according to which frontier fighting was to be conducted. These rules, which were ignored by the tribes, set up 'proscribed areas' inside which troops could not open fire on a party of

26. Transport and mountain batteries climbing down the Kohat Pass, 1897.

less than ten unless they were obviously armed; outside these areas troops could only open fire after having been shot at. The nature of the tribesmen's clothes made concealment of weapons easy and the troops' task even more difficult. Tribes continued to behead and mutilate troops who fell into their hands; troops therefore took few prisoners. The RAF was ordered to drop leaflets twenty-four hours before bombing any target.

1933   Mohmand activity, resulting from pressure by the Upper tribe on the Lower tribe to cut off relationship with the Government. Troops intervened and troubles stopped.

1934   On 5 April, at Kila Hari, one of the most ferocious fights in frontier history occurred; it lasted all night. On the 11th, the British and Indian troops launched a full-scale attack at Loe Agra and defeated the tribes.

1935   Further campaign against the Mohmands. Hitler sent 'technicians' to Afghanistan. Russia subsidized the Fakir of Ipi of the Waziris.

1936   The Fakir of Ipi threatened communications with Razmak: as his cause for fighting he took the 'Islam Bibi' case in which the wife of a Hindu merchant was abducted and forced to marry a Waziri in a Muslim ceremony; the Hindu husband sued in court and won.

1937   Over 30,000 troops fighting against the fakir, whose followers skilfully used the Durand Line, taking refuge behind it after their raids, kidnapping, burnings and murders, knowing that the British could not cross it.

Fakir's HQ eventually taken, but the fakir had fled.

1938 On 23 July, the fakir attacked Bannu at night, killing 200 civilians and doing immense damage.

Hitler sent agents to disturb the frontier in order to keep as many British troops there as possible.

1939 Outbreak of Second World War, during which time the Frontier was relatively quiet.

To the tribes on the Frontier, Independence on 14 August 1947 was something of a puzzle. At first they were unable to understand why the British had left, after all they had not been defeated so why give up the land? By December the last soldier had left the great fortress of Razmak, which now stood silent and empty. The Fakir of Ipi tried again and again to stir up the tribes but was unsuccessful as many tribesmen went south towards Peshawar and found jobs and houses and a new life. But the Frontier and its problems was now no concern of the British.

Where East met West, just east of Port Said, in the late summer of 1947, an age-old ritual was carried out for the last time. Everyone on the ship bringing the troops back to England was paraded on deck and at a given signal they all flung their topees into the sea; and that was the last of India.

The Plates

A1 Sergeant, Bengal Horse Artillery, 1842
The artillery uniforms of the Presidencies of Bengal, Bombay and Madras were modelled on those of the Royal and Royal Horse Artillery. The undress cap is worn here with oilskin cover; the full-dress headgear was a superb black japanned helmet with flowing red horsehair mane. A native *poshteen* is worn over the blue jacket and overalls trimmed red and laced yellow; note that the centre row of the five rows of buttons is ball-shaped, and the four flanking rows are half-ball buttons. The red and

27. Men of the mountain batteries halting for water, Tirah 1897. The swords are reversed. (Wilkinson-Latham)

28. The Gordon Highlanders storming the Sempagha Pass. (Wilkinson-Latham)

29. Although nearly obsolete, these Hale's Rockets were used, but by all accounts the Afridis treated them with contempt. (Wilkinson-Latham)

yellow barrel sash has a red cord looped up to the right with a yellow acorn finial. A white crossbelt and waistbelt with brass fittings are worn, the latter with sabre-slings.

A2 Captain, 44th Foot, 1842
After the famous painting of Captain Souter at the last stand of the 44th at Gandamak. The undress forage cap is worn, with black on dark-blue embroidery and gold regimental number. Full-dress coatee and regulation trousers are worn with privately acquired boots and a *poshteen*; the weapons are the 1822-pattern gilt-hilted infantry sword, and a percussion pistol perhaps acquired from a horse-gunner. The Regimental Colour is wrapped round the officer's waist beneath the *poshteen* to save it from capture; on seeing this 'richly brocaded waistcoat' the Afghan tribesmen spared Souter's life and held him for ransom—with such clothes he was obviously a man of means!

A3 Private of a battalion company, 44th Foot, 1842
This soldier wears the rather vulgar-looking regulation dress of a line infantryman of the period, which falls uneasily between the classic Napoleonic Wars style and the neater simplicity of later Victorian uniforms. The coatee chest bears white, square-ended, singly-spaced button-loops of graduated length, and the collar, in facing colour, is decorated with a long button-loop. The cuffs are also in facing, and the buttons are pewter. Centre companies wore a mean-looking epaulette, a strap of facing edged and fringed white; the tuft of the bell-topped shako is also in the centre company form of white over red. Flank companies wore a grenade or a bugle-horn over the number on the shako plate.

B1 Officer, 3rd Light Dragoons, 1842
The bell-top shako is covered with white quilted calico, the cap-lines being tied over this. Other ranks wore double-breasted full-dress coatees, and officers this shell-jacket—it fastened internally with hooks and eyes and the numerous 'buttons' are merely decorative beads. The laced crossbelt is of regimental design—gold lace with scarlet train and silver furniture; it carried at the back a silver-faced box-pouch bearing a gilt crowned VR cypher in the centre, the flap edge having foliate engraving.

30. 'The Disaster of the Dorset Regiment, hand to hand fighting with the enemy in a nullah'. Sketch by *Illustrated London News* war artist Melton Prior.

The black undress belt had a snake fastening and five slings—one short and one long for the sabre, and three long for the plain black patent leather undress sabretache.

B2 Private, 13th Foot, 1842
The peaked forage cap was sometimes worn with a white cover and curtain, sometimes with a cover alone; regimental numbers were normally painted or sewn to the front. This soldier wears the undress fatigue jacket with regimental facings, and white summer trousers. Crossbelt equipment is still worn. The weapon could be either the 1839 conversion of the Brown Bess, or the new 1842 percussion pattern; both had the traditional triangular socket bayonet.

B3 Sepoy, Light Company, 35th Bengal Native Infantry, 1842
The traditional peakless shako of the Company's Army, bound with yellow lace and with chin-scales tied up, has the green ball-tuft of the light company. Essentially similar to that of the British

soldier of the day, the red coatee has the 'wings' of a flank company. Trousers were white in summer, grey in winter. The equipment was the same as that used in the British Army, but the weapon was still the old India-Pattern flintlock Brown Bess—native troops had not converted to percussion muskets at this date.

C1 Private, 10th Hussars, 1879

This trooper wears campaign dress of the second Afghan War—foreign service helmet; India-pattern khaki drill service tunic with brass buttons, stand collar, breast pockets and no rear vents; striped home service overalls and puttees. The crossbelt bears the carbine ammunition pouch, and the waistbelt the sabre-slings.

C2 Officer, 18th Foot attached Commissariat, Kabul, 1880

The undress forage cap has a netted button and tracing on the crown, and an embroidered crowned harp badge above the regimental number on the band, which is in a black-on-dark-blue shamrock

31. Filtering water before adding it to the required stimulant—Scotch being the favourite. From left to right: Melton Prior, Major Hamilton, and Major Mercer with, standing, General Spragg. Note the variety of headdress. (Wilkinson-Latham)

32. Gordon Highlanders burying their dead after the Battle of Dargai. Spine pads were for protection from the heat. (Wilkinson-Latham)

pattern. The khaki tunic and breeches are obviously privately purchased to the officer's own design—note the khaki twist shoulder cords. The khaki puttees have blue tie-tapes. The equipment includes a crossbelt to support a sword, and a revolver holster and pouch; there was no regulation pattern of officer's field equipment at this date, and photographs show many variations.

C3 Infantry officer, 1879
The extraordinary 'Colind hat' was invented by Henry Hart of Oxford Street, London; made in straw with a cloth cover, it had an internal headband which allowed all-round ventilation. Though practical, it was—for obvious reasons—never popular. Like the last figure, this officer is painted from a contemporary photograph. The uniform may have been a locally-dyed white outfit. The leather equipment includes a scabbard with nickle mounts for the 1822 sword with 1846 modified 'Wilkinson' blade; and a holster and pouch worn on the waistbelt.

D1 Officer, Royal Horse Artillery, 1879
Again painted from a photograph, this officer wears an undress 'pill-box' cap with gold lace band, netted button and tracing on the crown. The khaki tunic with breast pockets and cloth belt conceals the belt from which hang the five slings for the 1822 light cavalry sabre and the black undress sabre-tache with gilt badge. The full-dress crossbelt is worn. The blue trousers, with a 2-in scarlet stripe, are tucked into spurred 'butcher boots'.

D2 Sowar, 12th Bengal Cavalry, 1888
The khaki *kurta*, worn with regimental shoulder-chains and cummerbund, is typical of the field service dress of the native cavalry regiments. The turban is of regimental pattern. Pale twill breeches are worn beneath the *kurta*, which is slit at each side seam. The Patterson equipment is worn, with ready-use ammunition in loops on the shoulder braces; these crossed at the back and supported the

33

Snider-Enfield ·577 carbine, the butt of which was held by the additional support strap seen passing round the hip. (By this time the ·455 Martini-Henry had been in use by British units for more than fifteen years.) The sword, carried in a frog, varied considerably from regiment to regiment; in the 12th it was stirrup-hilted with a curved 'Paget' blade, in a leather-covered wooden scabbard with steel fittings. The leather was selected according to the religion of regimental personnel—donkey skin was most popular.

D3 Havildar, Mountain Artillery Battery, 1889

The Indian mountain-gunners achieved a high reputation for efficiency, and the accurate supporting fire which their little screw-guns could deliver in even the most inaccessible terrain proved decisive in many a punitive expedition on the Frontier. This sergeant is shown in full dress of traditional artillery blue and red with yellow cord

34. A mountain battery 'screw-gun' in position ready to open fire. The barrel was carried in two pieces, and had to be screwed together before being mounted on the carriage, which was then put on the wheels. (Wilkinson-Latham)

decorations; in the field khaki would be worn, with a khaki turban fringed red. The battery number is displayed on the shoulder strap. The brown leather equipment includes a crossbelt with brass adjustment buckle, terminating in a frog on the left hip which carried the curved mountain artillery sword. This had a brass stirrup hilt, a blackened cast-iron grip and a single-edged blade, and was worn in a brown leather scabbard with brass locket and chape. It was carried 'in reverse' in the Russian fashion, with the cutting edge to the rear.

E1 Private, British Infantry, 1897

In India the foreign service helmet was worn with a *paggri*, showing here as a lump beneath the cloth cover; in the field, chinscales were replaced by a leather strap. The tunic had a stand collar (although a stand-and-fall collar was ordered the previous year) and two breast pockets. An extra flap was slipped over the left shoulder strap and fastened to the two top front buttons to protect the tunic from gun-oil stains. Cholera belts and spine pads were issued to all ranks, the latter being worn buttoned down the back of the tunic—this will be

Matching trousers were worn, tucked into puttees,
with black ankle boots. The equipment is the Slade
Wallace of 1888, with haversack and canteen; it
was dyed light khaki in the field. The weapon is the
magazine Lee-Metford with 1888-pattern short
sword bayonet. Note service chevrons and
marksman's badge.

E2 Havildar, 30th Punjab Infantry, 1897

The turban or *safa* is khaki drill, like the rest of the
uniform, with the regimental badge on the front.
The use of a senior NCO's red sash in the field is
puzzling, but this figure is prepared from a
contemporary photograph. The arrangement of
the kit is also untypical. What is clear is that he
wears the Slade Wallace adaptation for Indian
troops, who were still armed with the single-shot
Martini-Henry, with two pouches and shoulder
braces in brown leather. The 1887 Martini-Henry
Mk III sword bayonet was worn on the left side in a
frog and a steel-tipped scabbard.

**35. Infantry with Afridi spies. Note the infantry dress with
shoulder flap to protect the tunic from rifle oil. (Wilkinson-
Latham)**

E3 Sowar, 10th Bengal Lancers, 1897

This trooper wears the regimental *paggri* and *kullah*
headgear, the *paggri* being worn to show a 'fan' at
the left. The service dress *kurta* is unremarkable; it is
worn with lighter drill breeches and black puttees.
In the 10th the sword had a three-bar hilt for
troopers; it was worn in a frog suspended from the
belt on two straps. The 9-ft bamboo India-pattern
lance has a ball finial and a hollow-ground
triangular-section head.

F1 War correspondent, 1897

This represents Melton Prior, the famous *Illustrated
London News* artist, in his privately assembled
campaign dress for the 1897 Frontier operations; a
cord jacket and breeches are worn with leather
leggings and boots and the topi without which no
Englishman would brave the tropics. After bitter
experiences Prior carefully marked his essential
campaign rations—champagne, port, other assor-

ted wines, whisky, and 1,000 cigarettes—as 'Drawing Material'. His admiration of the British soldier did not blind him to Tommy's acquisitive habits.

F2 Private, 1st Gordon Highlanders, 1908
Prepared from a photograph, this figure wears drill order—'greyback' shirt with aproned kilt, puttees, and the Wolesley helmet introduced for other ranks in 1904. In full dress a white version was worn, with chinscales. The odd-looking combination of equipment is the 1903 bandolier pattern, in this case worn with the full-dress white Slade-Wallace belt; the four belt-pouches and the five bandolier pouches carry clip ammunition for the Short Magazine Lee-Enfield introduced in 1903. The

1903 bayonet is carried in a white Slade-Wallace frog on the left; with the more usual brown belt the frog would also be brown.

F3 Officer, South Wales Borderers, 1937

This officer wears the khaki drill shirt beneath a khaki woollen pullover, with the shirt shoulder straps protruding to display ranking. Bedford cord breeches, puttees and ankle boots complete the uniform. The equipment is the 1937 Mills pattern officers' set with belt, shoulder braces, holster, ammunition and binocular pouches, and a small pack on the left side.

G1 Highland Guard, Afghan Army, 1879

Photographs confirm the Gilbert & Sullivan appearance of this unit, who were dressed in cast-off and modified British Army items purchased locally. The scarlet 'doublet' is of dubious provenance, and is enlivened by a yellow collar and 'Inverness skirts'. The 'kilt' in pleated white and red cloth is worn over pantaloons with leather

38. An Afridi tribesman sheltering behind a rock, about to 'snipe' a target. Unfortunately for this posed Afridi, he has no flint to the damaged lock of his *jezail* and he has failed to cock it. (National Army Museum)

39. Picket of North-West Frontier Constabulary, 1920; they are observing the movement of an advancing column. (National Army Museum)

40. Officers of the South Wales Borderers in campaign dress on the 'Grim' in 1937. Note the Mills equipment. (South Wales Borderers)

anklets and boots. The white crossbelt supports a pouch at the rear, and another is slung on the right of the waistbelt.

G2 Cavalry trooper, Afghan Army, 1879
The rather unbecoming headgear was of black felt, and the uniform tunic and trousers were of scarlet and black respectively, with high boots. Equipment included a crossbelt with pouch for carbine ammunition, and a narrow shoulder belt for the stirrup-hilted light cavalry sabre, which was slung in the Russian fashion, in a steel scabbard.

G3 Amir Ayub Khan, 1880
The Amir wore a heavy beaten brass helmet in imitation of the British Albert-pattern cavalry helmet, with white feather plumes, oakleaf strip decoration on front, back and peak, and a badge featuring oak and laurel leaves surrounding a cut star. The white uniform was lavishly laced with gold, and the *shamshir* had a silver-mounted red velvet scabbard, an ebony grip and a gold and crimson knot.

H Frontier tribesmen
The clothing worn by the Pathans varied from tribe to tribe, but the basic garments were the *angarka*—loose blouse—and baggy trousers, usually of off-white cotton. Headgear consisted of the *kullah*, the pointed overstitched cap, round which the *lungi* was tied to form a loose turban. The *lungi* could also be worn as a waist-sash. In cold weather the reversed goatskin *poshteen* was normally worn; its amount of embroidery depended on wealth and status. The Waziris tended to favour a dark-red or indigo turban and a dark-red or pink waist-sash. The Kurram Valley tribes wore an *angarka* of dark blue with white patches similar to the dress of Sudanese dervishes. Khyber Pass Afridis usually wore a grey or blue *angarka* with off-white trousers. Tribes often adopted a predominant but by no means uniform combination of colours.

Besides the captured rifles which were the constant and most valuable form of booty and currency on the Frontier from the early nineteenth century to the present day, tribes who were not sustained by British subsidies made do with the matchlock muzzle-loading *jezail*; this cumbersome weapon, whose burning slowmatch had obvious disadvantages for night combat, was surprisingly accurate in the hands of an experienced warrior. As time went by, those tribes who could afford them bought European—mainly British—rifles; by 1908 most tribesmen sported a Martini-Henry, and the luckier (or more skilled thieves) carried the occasional Lee-Metford or Lee-Enfield. The skill and cunning of lone warriors who wormed their way into British encampments at night to steal weapons was legendary; soldiers always slept with their rifles chained to their bodies or chained together, and the bolts of the magazine rifles were often removed at night. The tribal craftsmen were incredibly skilful at reproducing European weapons with the most primitive of tools; they were not equal to making an SMLE bolt, but if one could be stolen they were capable of building a rifle around it to a standard of workmanship which stands up to all but the closest examination.

Apart from firearms, the tribesmen were armed with a variety of edged weapons such as the *tulwar* sabre, the razor-sharp triangular-bladed Afghan knife in a range of sizes, and the punch-dagger illustrated. Swordsmen were often protected by a round shield, either of engraved metal work or of heavy leather with metal bosses and studs.

INDEX

Figures in **bold** refer to illustrations.

Abdur Rahman, Amir of Afghanistan 17, 22
Afghan Army **4**, 37–8, **G1**, **G2**
Afghanistan
 British occupation (1839–42) 5–12
 British occupation (1878–81) 14–17
 Dost Mahomed's deposure 4, 6
 planned invasion of India (1919) 23
 Russian invasion (1885) 17
 threat from Persia 3, 4, 12
air operations 24, 26, 27, 28
Akbar Khan 10, 12
Amanullah Khan, Amir of Afghanistan 23, 24
Amir-ul-Mulk, ruler of Chitral 18
Amritsar massacre (1919) 23
Arhanga Pass 21
Ayub Khan, Amir of Afghanistan **9**, 15, 16, 17, 38, **G3**

Bala Hissar 6, 8–9, **14**
Bannu, attack on (1938) 29
Beymaroo Hills, British attack on (1841) 9–10
Black Mountain expedition (1888) 17
Blood, Maj. Gen. Sir Bindon 20
Browne, Lt. Gen. Sam 14
Brydon, Dr **7**, 11
Burnes, Capt. 3–4, 6, 7–8
Burrows, Gen. 16

Cavagnari, Sir Louis **9**, 15
Charasia, battle of (1879) 15
Chitral, siege of (1895) 18–19
Coke, Capt. 12
Colind hats 33, **C3**
communications **13**, 14, **27**
Cotton, Willoughby 6–7

Dargai, battles of (1897) 21, **32**
Dost Mahomed, Amir of Afghanistan 3–4, **3**, 6, 10, 12, 13
Durand Line 18, 28
Dyer, Brig. Gen. 23, 24

East India Company 5, 7
Edwards, Lt. 18–19
Elphinstone, Maj. Gen. William 7, 8, 10, 11, 12
equipment
 Mills **38**
 Patterson 17, 33–4, **D2**
 Slade Wallace 17, 35, 36–7, **E1**, **E2**, **F2**
Eyre, Lt. Vincent 9

Findlater, Piper 21
First Afghan War (1838–42) 4–11
First Sikh War (1845–46) 12
Fort Hari–Sing **27**
Fort Jamrud **26**
Fowler, Lt. 18–19

frontier tribesmen 3, 38–9, **H**
 Afridis 20, 21, 22, 27, 30, **35–7**, 38
 Akazais 17
 Baluchis 20
 campaigns against 12, 13, 17, 19–22
 Douranees 7
 Ghilzais 7
 independence struggles 25–9
 Mahsuds 25
 Mohmands 21, 28
 Pathans 3, **8**, 19–20, 21, 25
 strengths and weapons 19–20, 38–9, **H**
 subsidies cut 7
 Waziris 18, 20, 25, 28, 38

Gandamak, 44th's last stand at (1842) **6**, 11, 31
Germany, and Afghanistan 28, 29
Ghaffar Khan, Abdul 25–7
Ghuznee, storming of (1839) **5**, 6

Habibullah Khan, Amir 22
Hamilton, Maj. **32**
Hensman, Philip 15–16
Herat 3, 4, 12

Indian Army: campaign armies and forces
 Bombay and Bengal Armies 4–11
 Kandahar Field Force 14

Kurram Field Force (later Kabul Field Force) **13**, 14–16
Peshawar Valley Field Force 14
Indian Army: subdivisions
1st Brigade 7, 9
3rd Light Dragoons 31, **B1**
3rd Royal Artillery 11
5th Light Cavalry 11
9th (Queen's Royal) Lancers **17**
10th Hussars 32, **C1**
13th Foot 31, **B2**
15th Cureton's Multanis **23**
15th/19th Hussars 27
20th Lancers 27
44th Foot **6**, 10, 11, 31, **A2, A3**
66th Regiment 16, 17
72nd Highlanders 14
Bengal Cavalry 23–4, **D2**
Bengal Horse Artillery 29–31, **A1**
Bengal Lancers **19**, 35, **E3**
Bengal Native Infantry **22**, 31–2, **B3**
Bombay Grenadiers 16
Central India Horse **20, 25**
Derbyshire Regiment 21
Dorsetshire Regiment 21, 31
Gordon Highlanders 19, 21, **26, 30, 32**, 36–7, **F2**
Guides 19, **24**, 27
Gurkhas 14, 21, **21**
infantry 33, 34–5, **35, C3, E1**
Kashmiri light infantry 18
Kashmiri Sappers 19
King's Own Scottish Borderers 19
mountain batteries **28, 29**, 34, **34, D3**
Punjab Infantry **12**, 35, **E2**
Royal Horse Artillery 9, 10–11, 33, **D1**
Sikhs 4, 18, 19, 21
Somerset Light Infantry 23
South Wales Borderers 37, **38, F3**
Ipi, Fakir of 28–9
Islam Bibi case 28

Jalalabad 7, **7**, 9, 10, 12
Josephs, Mr **13**
Jubbar Khan 6

Kabul **12, 14**
bombed by British (1919) 24
British occupations 6, 7–10, **14**, 15–17
Kandahar 5–6, 10, 16, 17, **17**
Kelly, Lt. Col. James 19
Khyber Pass 20–1, 22
Kila Hari, battle of (1934) 28
Kohat Pass **28**

Landi Kotal 23, **36**
Lockhart, Sir William 21
Loe Agra, battle of (1934) 28
Low, Maj. Gen. Sir Robert 18

Macnaghten, Sir William Henry 4–5, 6, 7, 8, 10
MacPherson (war correspondent) 14–15
Mad Mullah 20
Maiwand, battle of (1880) 16
Malakand 19, 20
marches, column disposition **10**
medals 22
Mercer, Maj. **32**

Nadir Khan 24
Nizam-ul-Mulk, ruler of Chitral 18
North-West Frontier Constabulary **37**

Persia, and Afghanistan 3, 4, 12
Peshawar, disturbances in (1930) 25–6, 27
poshteens **15, 38, H**
Primrose, Maj. Gen. 16
Prior, Melton 31, **32, 33**, 35–6, **F1**
Punjab uprising (1919) 23

Ranjit Singh 4
Razmak 25, 29
Red Shirts(Khudai Khitmatgers) 25–7
Reshun 18–19
Roberts, Brig. Abraham 6–7
Roberts, Lord 6, 14–17, **15**
Robertson, Surgeon Major 18
Russia, and Afghanistan 3, 4, 13, 15, 17, 22, 28

Sale, Lady 9, 11
Sale, Sir Robert 7, 9
Second Afghan War (1878–80) 13–17
Sempagha Pass 21, **30, 33**
Shelton, Brig. 8–9, 9–10
Sher Afzal 18
Sher Ali, Amir of Afghanistan 13, 15, **18**
Sherpur, battle of (1879) 16
Sind 5, 12
Souter, Capt. **6**, 11, 31, **A2**
Spragg, Gen. **32**
The Standard (newspaper) 14–15, 21
Stewart, Maj. Gen. Sir Donald 14, 16
'Stonehenge Ridge' 23–4
Shuja, Shah 4, 6, 7, 12
Suja-ul-Mulk, ruler of Chitral 18
Swat Valley uprising (1897) 20–1

Thal 24
Third Afghan War (1919) 22–5
Tirah 21–2, 26–7

Udney, Sir Richard **36**
Umra Khan, ruler of Jandol 18–19

Victoria, Queen of Great Britain and Ireland 20–1, 22

war correspondents 14–15, 15–16, 31, **32, 33**, 35–6, **F1**
Waziristan 18, 25
weapons
artillery 19, **34**
bayonets 35, 37, **A3, E1, E2, F2**
carbines 17, **19**, 34, **D2**
Hale's Rockets 30
jezails **8**, 9, **16, 37, 38, H**
lances **20**, 35, **E3**
muskets 31–2, **B2, B3**
punch-daggers 39, **H**
rifles **16**, 18, 19–20, **21**, 35, 38–9, **E1, E2**
sabres 38, **G2**
swords 17, **19, 20, 29**, 33, 34, 35, **C3, D2, D3, E3**
tribesmen 19–20, 38–9, **H**